NATIONAL
GEOGRAPHIC
KiDS

weird
but
true!

8

350 OUTRAGEOUS FACTS

NATIONAL GEOGRAPHIC
WASHINGTON, D.C.

An **earthquake** made **Mount Everest** about an **inch shorter.**

(2.5 cm)

4

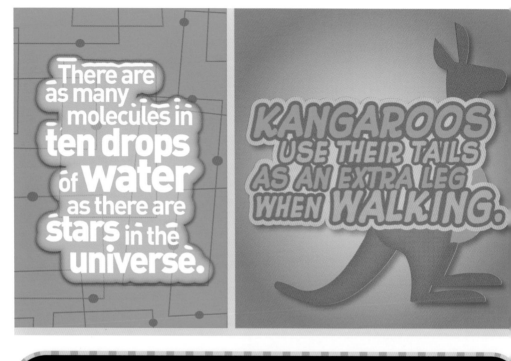

There are as many molecules in **ten drops** of **water** as there are **stars** in the **universe.**

KANGAROOS USE THEIR TAILS AS AN EXTRA LEG WHEN WALKING.

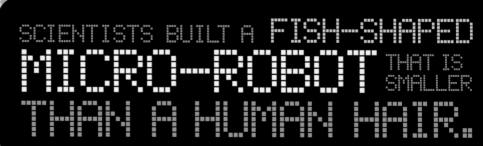

SCIENTISTS BUILT A FISH-SHAPED **MICRO-ROBOT** THAT IS SMALLER THAN A HUMAN HAIR.

A **FARMER** FROM MASSACHUSETTS, U.S.A., **ONCE PADDLED DOWN A RIVER IN AN** **817-POUND** (371-kg) **HOLLOWED-OUT PUMPKIN.**

MORE PEOPLE ARE KILLED EACH YEAR BY DOMESTIC PIGS THAN BY SHARKS.

A compound in **human spit** can help **heal wounds.**

Scientists use a **barfing machine** and fake vomit to help them study how **viruses** spread through the air.

The planet Mercury is shrinking.

LUKE SKYWALKER'S **LIGHTSABER** HAS ACTUALLY BEEN TO **SPACE.**

ONE MAN OWNS 500,000 PIECES OF *STAR WARS*

The sound of **Darth Vader's breathing** was inspired by breathing apparatuses used for **scuba diving.**

A WATERFALL IN MINNESOTA, U.S.A., DROPS INTO A DEEP HOLE AND DISAPPEARS.

A GIANT BLACK HOLE ATE A STAR AND BURPED OUT A FLAME.

SOME OF THE EARLIEST BOATS WERE MADE FROM PLANTS.

Dragonflies can fly straight up and down and hover in midair like a helicopter.

A NOW EXTINCT FROG SPECIES SWALLOWED ITS EGGS, INCUBATED THEM IN ITS STOMACH, AND GAVE BIRTH THROUGH ITS MOUTH.

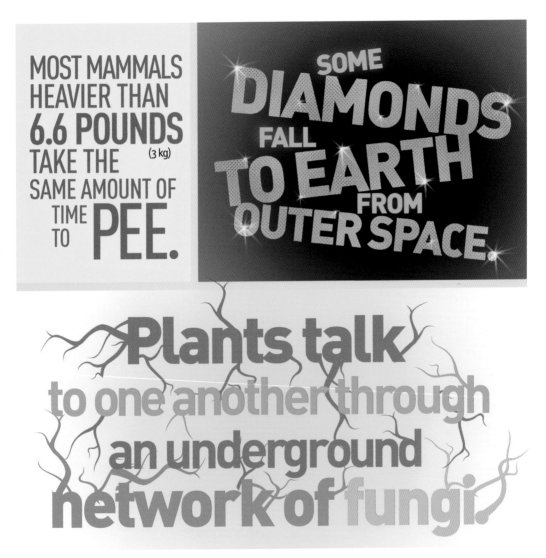

MOST MAMMALS HEAVIER THAN **6.6 POUNDS** (3 kg) TAKE THE SAME AMOUNT OF TIME TO **PEE.**

SOME **DIAMONDS** FALL **TO EARTH** FROM **OUTER SPACE**

Plants talk to one another through **an underground network of fungi.**

YOU NEED A **FOOT-LONG STICK,** (0.3-m) A **THREE-POUND PUCK,** (1.4-kg) AND **SNORKEL GEAR** TO **PLAY** UNDERWATER HOCKEY.

ONLY ABOUT **10 PERCENT** OF THE POPULATION IS LEFT-HANDED.

Drinking *coffee* in 17th-century *Turkey* was punishable by *death.*

YOUR BODY'S SMELL—OR "**ODORPRINT**"—IS AS UNIQUE AS YOUR FINGERPRINTS.

WEEEE!

As part of a **beaver-relocation effort,** **76 beavers** once **parachuted** into the Idaho, U.S.A., wilderness.

Raindrops are shaped like pancakes.

SCIENTISTS SAY YOUR **GUT** HAS A "BRAIN."

Ants give themselves **medicine** when they get sick.

Lightning almost never strikes the North or South Poles.

LIGHTNING **STRIKES** MEN MORE OFTEN THAN IT DOES WOMEN.

NEWBORN TASMANIAN DEVILS ARE THE SIZE OF A RAISIN.

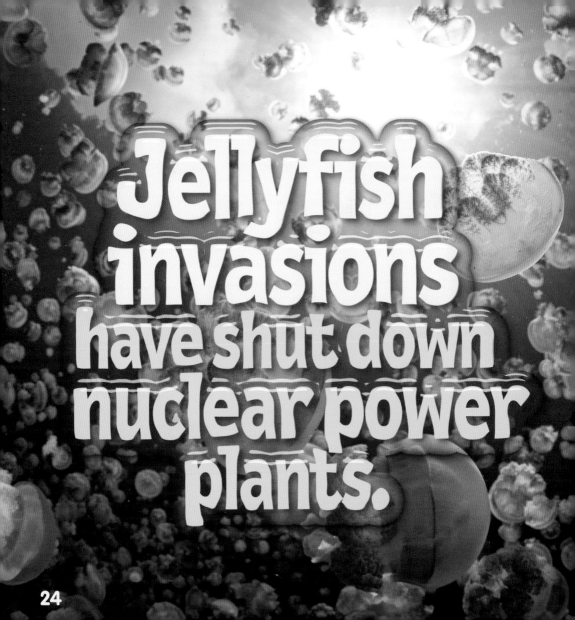

Jellyfish invasions have shut down nuclear power plants.

There's an app that lets people **rent** out their **toilets.**

SCIENTISTS FOUND **PREHISTORIC VIRUSES** IN **SIBERIAN ICE.**

A 16th-century *astronomer* lost part of his **nose** in a duel about *math.*

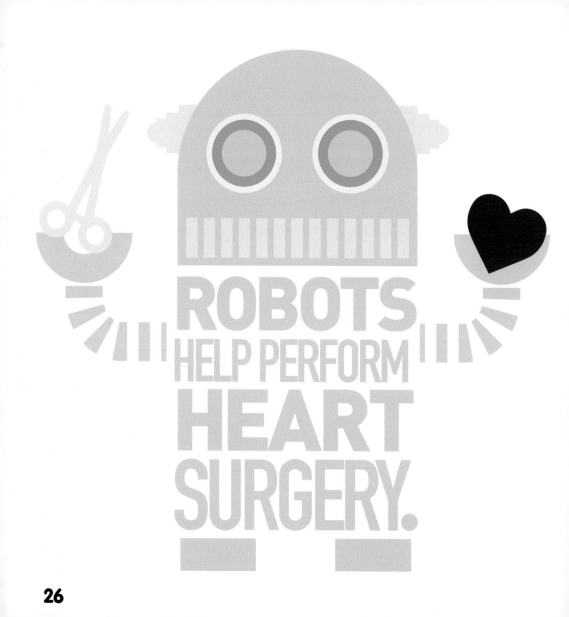

ROBOTS
HELP PERFORM
HEART
SURGERY.

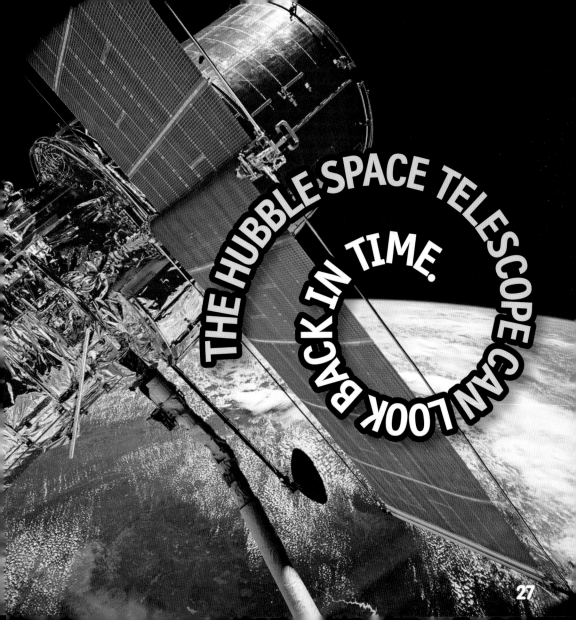

THE HUBBLE SPACE TELESCOPE CAN LOOK BACK IN TIME.

27

Mushrooms are also called toadstools.

NEANDERTHALS FLOSSED THEIR TEETH WITH TWIGS AND BLADES OF GRASS.

peecycling = using urine to fertilize vegetables

RESEARCHERS HAVE DEVELOPED 3-D GLASSES FOR INSECTS.

A STUDY FOUND THAT CHILDREN WHOSE FAMILIES WASH DISHES BY HAND HAVE FEWER ALLERGIES THAN KIDS WHOSE FAMILIES USE A DISHWASHER.

Wolf pups can't see or hear when they're born.

You are made of star dust.

Some plants can hear themselves being eaten.

There was only one student in New Mexico State University's first graduating class.

There are approximately **3 trillion** (3,000,000,000,000) trees on Earth.

ONE RARE PLANT GROWS ONLY ON TOP OF DIAMOND DEPOSITS.

THAT'S WEIRD!

A **BROWN BAT** CAN EAT **1,000 MOSQUITOES** IN AN HOUR.

People in one small Turkish town communicate over long distances by **whistling.**

A MAN SUED THE KELLOGG COMPANY BECAUSE HE FOUND NO REAL FRUIT IN HIS FROOT LOOPS CEREAL.

SCIENTISTS THINK **T. REX** WAS A CANNIBAL.

38

Some **carnivorous plants** can **eat** birds.

During his 1905 U.S. presidential inauguration, Teddy Roosevelt *wore a ring* containing a lock of **Abraham Lincoln's** *hair.*

Your brain produces enough **energy to** power a **small lightbulb.**

HUMMINGBIRDS USE **HAWKS** FOR PROTECTION.

moonbow=

a nighttime rainbow

Early **rugby balls** were made from **inflated pigs' bladders.**

2015 was the International Year of Light.

SCIENTISTS HAVE DISCOVERED A PROTEIN THAT CAN PREVENT ICE CREAM FROM MELTING QUICKLY IN HOT WEATHER.

THE BOARD GAME
MONOPOLY
WAS ORIGINALLY CALLED
THE LANDLORD'S GAME.

MONOPOLY
IS BASED ON
STREET NAMES
IN ATLANTIC CITY,
NEW JERSEY, U.S.A.

THE AVERAGE PERSON EATS **2,500** CALORIES AT THANKSGIVING DINNER.

Scientists who are Star Wars fans nicknamed a new species of ape the Skywalker hoolock gibbon.

There is NO WORD in the English language that RHYMES WITH "**month.**"

GRIMA = THE FEELING YOU GET WHEN YOU HEAR **FINGERNAILS** ON A CHALKBOARD

NASA found evidence that one of Saturn's moons has an energy source that may be able to **support life.**

Scientists found **152-million-year-old crocodile eggs** in Portugal.

Musicians have slightly **faster reaction times** than nonmusicians, a study found.

THERE IS A PLANT CALLED **JACK-GO-TO-BED-AT-NOON.**

Citizens of the town of Onoway, Canada, once had **PINK TAP WATER.**

Eels use Earth's magnetic field **to navigate.**

SCIENTISTS CREATED **ARTIFICIAL SKIN** THAT CAN **SENSE TEMPERATURE CHANGES.**

UPS drivers **hardly** ever make **left turns.**

In **6.7** million **years, a day will be** ONE MINUTE **LONGER.**

That's Weird!

Parrots, sea anemones, and mussels **don't toot.**

(But bats, hedgehogs, and snakes do.)

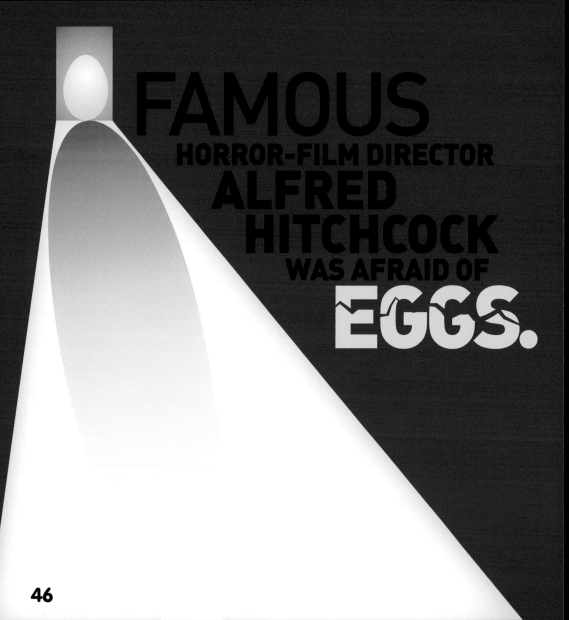

FAMOUS **HORROR-FILM DIRECTOR** ALFRED HITCHCOCK **WAS AFRAID OF** EGGS.

U.S. president James A. Garfield was fond of **squirrel soup.**

FEMALE **PHARAOHS** WORE FAKE BEARDS.

Scientists made medicine out of cockroach brain cells.

SAY WHAT?!

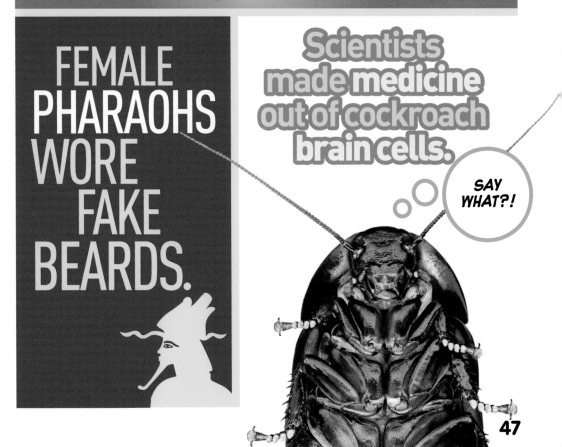

Elephants have "fingers" on the end of their trunks.

POPE LEO X **BURIED** HIS

SOME OF AN ELEPHANT'S **TEETH** ARE THE SIZE OF A BRICK.

PET ELEPHANT **UNDER** THE VATICAN.

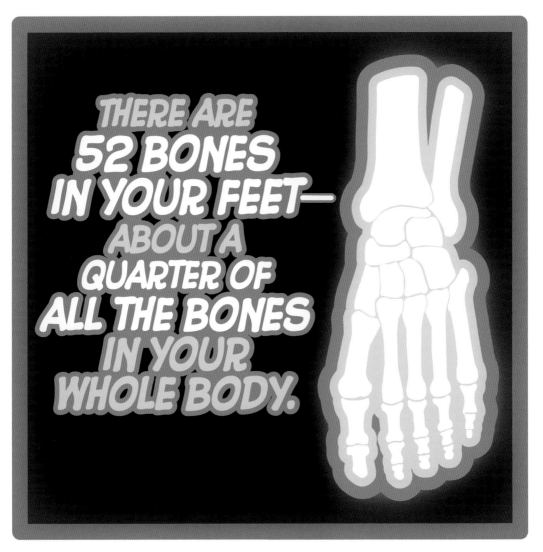

THERE ARE 52 BONES IN YOUR FEET— ABOUT A QUARTER OF ALL THE BONES IN YOUR WHOLE BODY.

VANILLA IS USED TO MAKE CHOCOLATE.

Some **dogs' paws** smell like **corn chips.**

AFTER THEIR 1972 NATIONAL HOCKEY LEAGUE WIN, THE BOSTON BRUINS'S NAME WAS MISSPELLED "BQSTQN BRUINS" ON THE STANLEY CUP.

THERE'S A ROCK ON MARS THAT LOOKS LIKE A FLOATING SPOON.

AN EAR OF CORN CAN HAVE UP TO 1,200 KERNELS.

A LIBROCUBICULARIST IS SOMEONE WHO READS IN BED.

53

Police "arrested" a goat for loitering outside a doughnut shop in Saskatchewan, Canada.

There are more than **40,000** types of rice.

If you strung together all the **cranberries** grown in North America **in one year,** they would stretch from Boston to Los Angeles, U.S.A., more than **500 times.**

SHEEP SHEARING IS A COMPETITIVE SPORT.

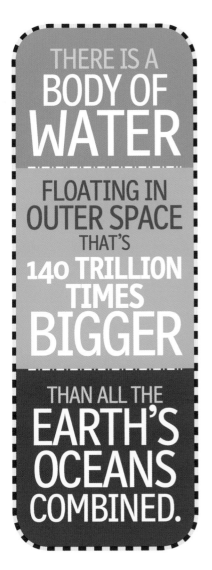

THERE IS A **BODY OF WATER** FLOATING IN OUTER SPACE THAT'S **140 TRILLION TIMES BIGGER** THAN ALL THE **EARTH'S OCEANS** COMBINED.

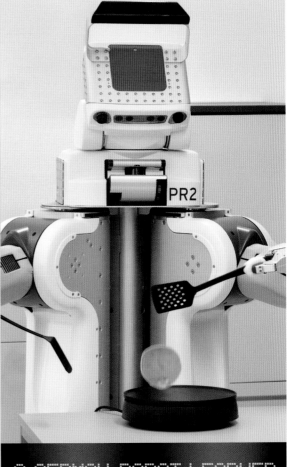

PR2

A GERMAN ROBOT LEARNED HOW TO MAKE PANCAKES.

penny farthing= a bicycle with a giant **front wheel** and a tiny back wheel

TOMATOES CAN BE PURPLE.

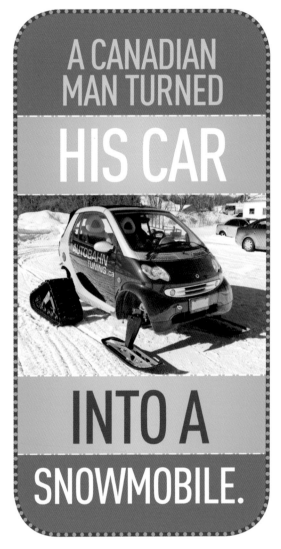

A CANADIAN MAN TURNED

HIS CAR

INTO A

SNOWMOBILE.

Fastest one-mile run (1.6-km) by a human wearing swim fins: 5 minutes and 48.86 seconds

During Olympic training, **swimmer** Michael Phelps consumed more than **12,000 calories** a day—about the equivalent of **80 cups of whole milk.** (18.9 L)

CHRISTOPHER COLUMBUS BROUGHT THE FIRST **LEMON SEEDS** TO THE AMERICAS.

PARTS OF CALIFORNIA, U.S.A., ARE SINKING.

IN NEW ZEALAND, PARENTS AREN'T ALLOWED TO NAME THEIR BABIES AFTER PUNCTUATION MARKS.

" ! ? ; - , (:) [,] ' { . . . }.

A HONEYBEE HAS THE SAME NUMBER OF HAIRS AS A SQUIRREL: THREE MILLION.

HONEY HAS BEEN FOUND IN THE CENTER OF OLD GOLF BALLS.

THAT COULD ARTIFICIALLY POLLINATE CROPS.

67

There's a **comet** shaped like a **rubber duck.**

CHOCOLATE WAS ONCE USED AS MONEY.

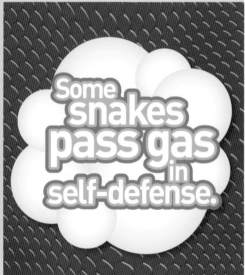

Some **snakes pass gas** in **self-defense.**

Painting was once an Olympic event.

One in four medicines comes from rain forest plants.

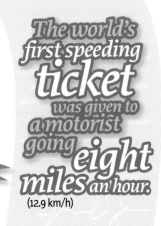

The world's first speeding **ticket** was given to a motorist going **eight miles** an hour.
(12.9 km/h)

The 1904 World's Fair featured a life-size elephant made of almonds.

BACTERIA TALK TO EACH OTHER.

"chicken wing" = a bad golf swing

The city of Redondo Beach, California, U.S.A., once chose a blimp as its official bird.

SNAILS SMELL WITH THEIR LIPS.

71

TO ENSURE THEY HAVEN'T BEEN SWITCHED OR TAMPERED WITH, ALL EGGS USED IN THE COMPETITIVE SPORT OF EGG THROWING ARE MARKED FOR SECURITY PURPOSES.

"FRIED EGG"=THE WAY A GOLF

SCIENTISTS HAVE FIGURED OUT HOW TO UNBOIL AN EGG.

BALL SOMETIMES LANDS IN A SAND TRAP

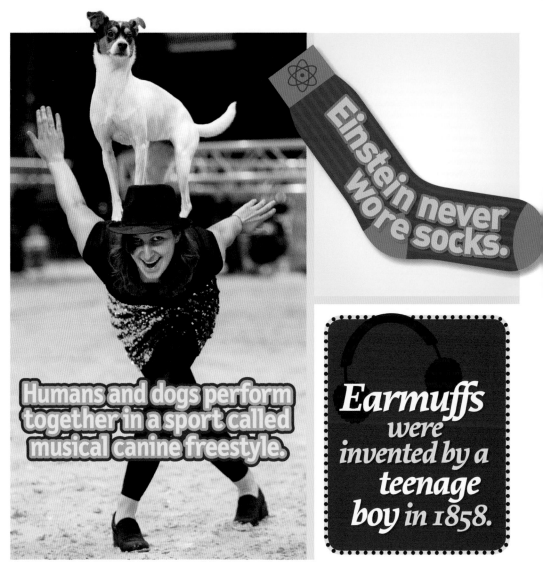

Einstein never wore socks.

Humans and dogs perform together in a sport called musical canine freestyle.

Earmuffs *were invented by a* **teenage boy** *in* 1858.

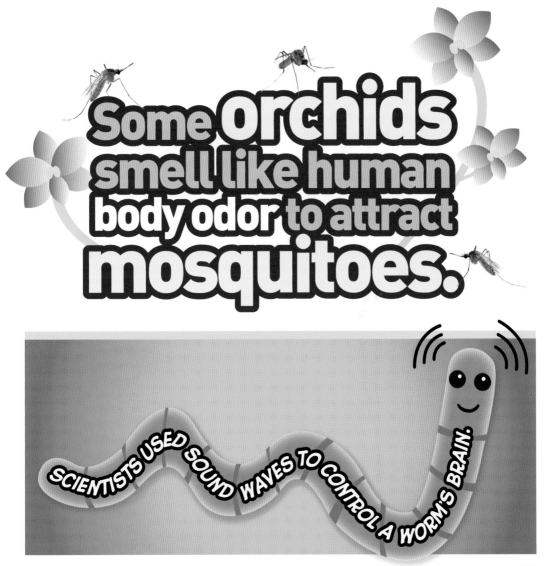

Some orchids smell like human body odor to attract mosquitoes.

SCIENTISTS USED SOUND WAVES TO CONTROL A WORM'S BRAIN.

DEATH METAL MUSIC ATTRACTS SHARKS.

IN NEW ZEALAND, YOU CAN **PLAY GOLF** WITH **FOOTBALL-SHAPED** GOLF BALLS.

Some scientists think that **plants** can learn.

Spiders can build **webs** that are a half mile long. (0.8 km)

77

An artist created an **18-foot-long** (5.5-m) **Batmobile** out of more than **500,000** Lego bricks.

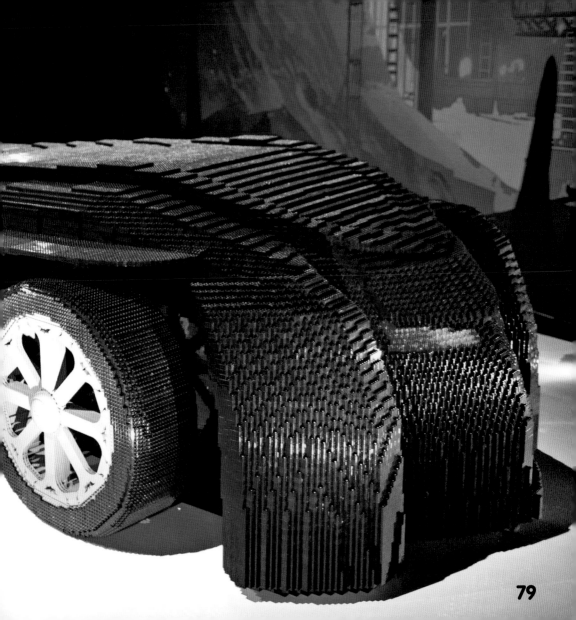

Tooth enamel evolved from ancient fish scales.

An aglet is the plastic piece at the end of your shoelace.

Fidgeting can make you healthier.

snood = the flesh that hangs down over a male turkey's beak

THE LONGEST PIZZA

EVER MADE WAS ALMOST A MILE LONG.
(1.6 km)

IT WAS MADE WITH

1.5 TONS
(1.4 t)
OF

MOZZARELLA

AND

2 TONS (1.8 t) OF

TOMATO SAUCE.

GLOBAL WARMING IS CHANGING THE SHAPE OF THE PLANET.

Kids grow faster in the springtime.

The **SLIME** of a frog found in southern India contains molecules that **CAN KILL THE FLU VIRUS.**

BIRD POOP HELPS FIGHT CLIMATE CHANGE **BY COOLING** DOWN **THE ARCTIC.**

People in a New Zealand town **built a tunnel** so the **penguins** that live there could **safely cross** under a busy road.

PENGUIN CROSSING

SOME WORMS CAN "TASTE" SUNLIGHT.

A **species of ant** in sub-Saharan Africa **rescues its wounded comrades** from battles with termites.

THE EASTER BUNNY SKYDIVED **INTO A NEIGHBORHOOD IN CORPUS CHRISTI, TEXAS, U.S.A.**

SCIENTISTS FOUND THE FOSSIL OF A **120-MILLION-**YEAR-OLD **FLYING DINOSAUR** WITH *IRIDESCENT FEATHERS.*

Coconut crabs **pinch harder than** grizzly bears bite.

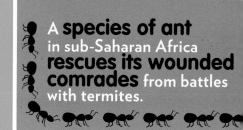

YELLOW TAXIS GET INTO **FEWER ACCIDENTS** THAN *BLUE ONES.*

A Minnesota, U.S.A., restaurant made a **100-pound** (45-kg) CHOCOLATE **EGG.**

Scientists invented a **SOLAR-POWERED DEVICE** that can **PULL WATER** from **DESERT AIR.**

That's Weird!

TALKING TO YOUR PUP IN A HIGH-PITCHED **"BABY VOICE"** HELPS IT PAY ATTENTION, **A STUDY FOUND.**

85

Bonobos **blOW** raspberries for attention.

LISTENING TO ROCK MUSIC WHILE EATING CAN MAKE FOOD TASTE SPICIER, ONE STUDY FOUND.

In China you can order dried-pork-and-seaweed-**flavored doughnuts.**

SOME **BABY SPIDERS** EAT THEIR MOTHER.

Computers can be programmed to recognize emotions in stories.

A **FROG** NAMED SANTJIE MADE THE **LONGEST RECORDED JUMP**— **33 FEET** 5.5 INCHES (10.2 m) AT A FROG DERBY IN **SOUTH AFRICA.**

The stringy parts of a banana are called phloem (FLO-em).

A **caterpillar's body** has **more muscles** than a human's.

baboon = a type of **lemon**

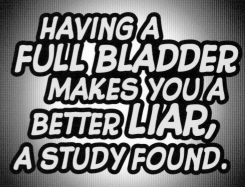

HAVING A *FULL BLADDER* MAKES YOU A BETTER *LIAR*, A STUDY FOUND.

ONE OF MARS'S MOONS IS FALLING APART.

Prairie dogs say hello with kisses.

VIRGA IS RAIN THAT EVAPORATES BEFORE IT HITS THE GROUND.

PLANTS CAN GET FEVERS.

A man named **Santa Claus** once ran for city council in North Pole, Alaska, U.S.A.

The average **tornado** is on the ground for only **five minutes.**

95

King Henry III
of England had a
pet bear
that swam in the
Thames River
and caught fish.

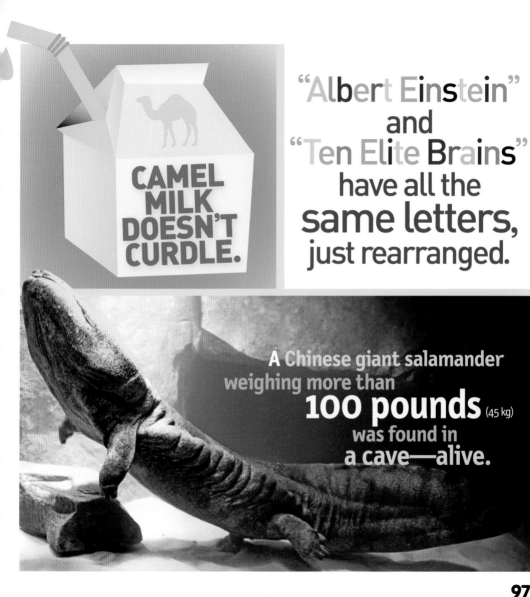

CAMEL MILK DOESN'T CURDLE.

"Albert Einstein" and "Ten Elite Brains" have all the **same letters,** just rearranged.

A Chinese giant salamander weighing more than **100 pounds** (45 kg) was found in a cave—alive.

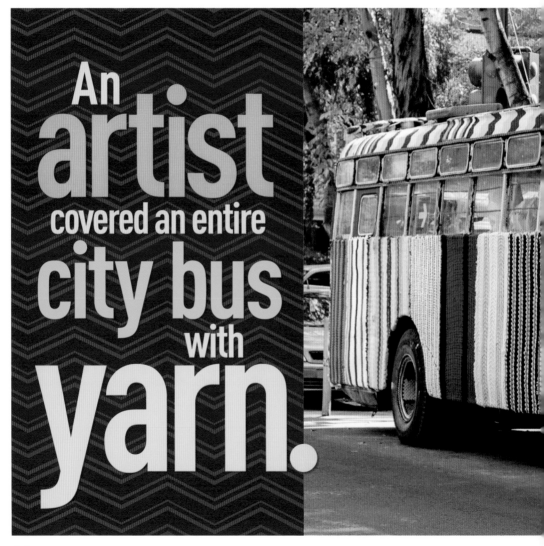

An **artist** covered an entire **city bus** with **yarn.**

扇沢一黒部ダム

Jousting is the *official sport*

of the U.S. state of Maryland.

PUMPKINS ALMOST WENT EXTINCT.

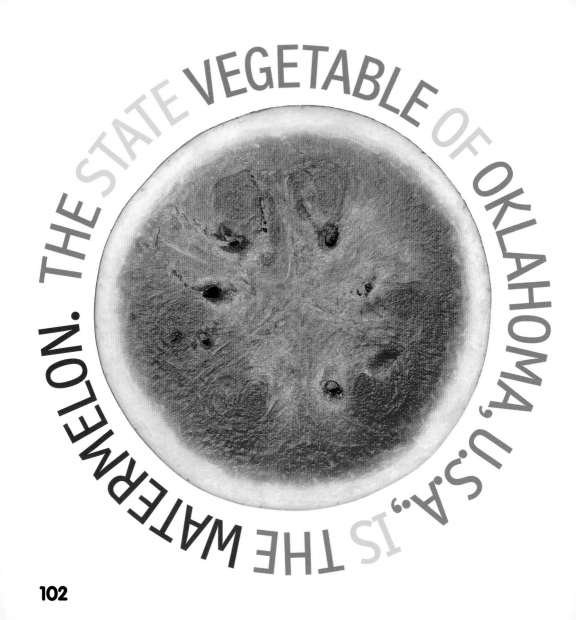

THE STATE VEGETABLE OF OKLAHOMA, U.S.A., IS THE WATERMELON.

The U.S. state of **Kansas** produces enough **wheat** every year to make **36 billion** loaves of bread.

HUMANS HAVE EXPLORED LESS

THAN 5 PERCENT OF THE OCEAN.

earworm = a song that gets stuck in your head

The first living things on Earth were **bacteria.**

DOMINOES' SPOTS ARE CALLED PIPS.

A man in Spain has ribs made by a 3-D printer.

THE SUN
SOMETIMES
HAS HOLES
IN IT.

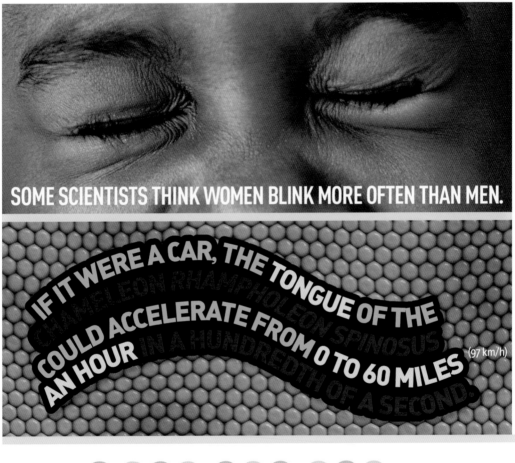

SOME SCIENTISTS THINK WOMEN BLINK MORE OFTEN THAN MEN.

IF IT WERE A CAR, THE TONGUE OF THE CHAMELEON RHAMPHOLEON SPINOSUS COULD ACCELERATE FROM 0 TO 60 MILES AN HOUR IN A HUNDREDTH OF A SECOND. (97 km/h)

ABOUT 9,000,000,000 PIECES OF

CANDY CORN WILL BE MADE THIS YEAR.

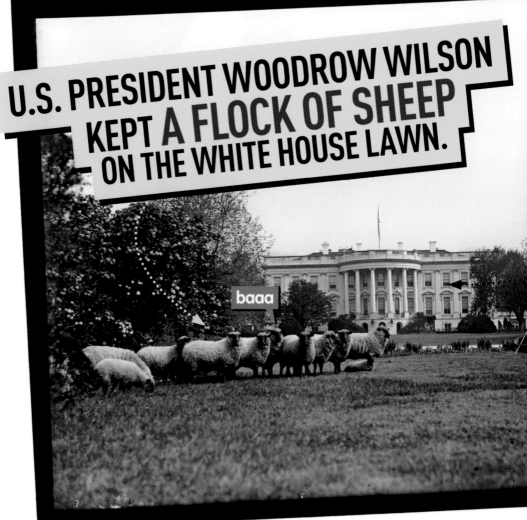

U.S. PRESIDENT WOODROW WILSON KEPT A FLOCK OF SHEEP ON THE WHITE HOUSE LAWN.

baaa

PRESIDENT
THEODORE ROOSEVELT
USED TO BOX
IN THE WHITE HOUSE.

PRESIDENT
ABRAHAM LINCOLN
PLAYED BASEBALL
ON THE WHITE HOUSE LAWN.

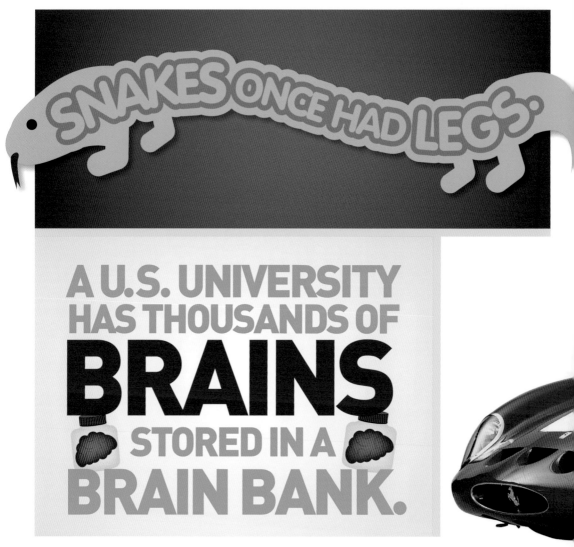

SNAKES ONCE HAD LEGS.

A U.S. UNIVERSITY HAS THOUSANDS OF **BRAINS** STORED IN A **BRAIN BANK.**

The most expensive **car** ever sold went for **$35.7 million.**

The
sea bunny
is actually
a slug.

PLUTO
IS ONLY ABOUT
HALF AS WIDE
AS THE
UNITED
STATES.

YOUR TASTE BUDS GO NUMB WHEN YOU FLY.

AMERICA'S FIRST ROLLER COASTER HAULED COAL IN THE MORNING AND PEOPLE IN THE AFTERNOON.

RESEARCHERS FOUND A NEW SPECIES OF **SPIDER THAT PLAYS PEEKABOO** TO ATTRACT MATES.

ONLY ONE PERCENT OF ALL THE **WATER** ON EARTH IS FIT FOR HUMAN USE.

No one really knows why **humans** have to **sleep.**

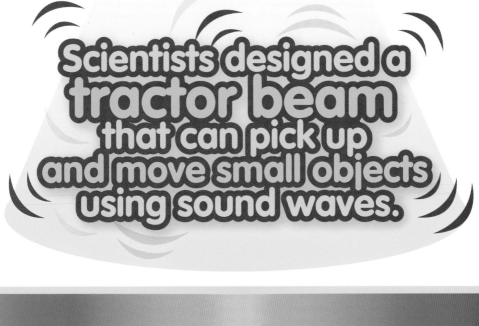

Scientists designed a **tractor beam** that can pick up and move small objects using sound waves.

THE EARTH IS MOVING AWAY FROM THE SUN.

YOUR **BRAIN** USES 20 PERCENT OF YOUR BODY'S **ENERGY** BUT MAKES UP ONLY 2 PERCENT OF YOUR BODY'S **WEIGHT.**

A CHINESE ASTRONOMER INVENTED AN **EARTHQUAKE DETECTOR** IN A.D. 132.

ONE SPECIES OF BIRD "TAP DANCES" TO ATTRACT A MATE.

I'VE GOT DANCIN' FEET!

A **ten-gallon cowboy hat** holds only three (2.8 L) quarts of water.

SOUR PATCH KIDS WERE ORIGINALLY CALLED MARS MEN.

AUTOMOBILES ARE THE

MOST **RECYCLED PRODUCT**
IN THE UNITED STATES.

123

There are about **3.4 trillion** gallons (13 trillion L) of water in **Earth's** atmosphere.

SCIENTISTS UNCOVERED FOSSILS FROM AN **ANCIENT GOOSELIKE BIRD** THAT WAS **FIVE FEET** (1.5 M) **TALL** AND WEIGHED **48 POUNDS** (22 KG).

A **650-YEAR-OLD** TEMPLE WAS DISCOVERED **UNDER A SUPERMARKET** IN MEXICO CITY.

FIREFIGHTERS IN DUBAI, U.A.E. WEAR **WATER-POWERED JET PACKS** TO FIGHT FIRES FROM THE AIR.

Dorado catfish migrate the length of the Amazon River and back: **7,200 miles** (11,587 km). (That's nearly the entire width of South America!)

SOME SCIENTISTS WANT TO **SPRAY GLACIERS** WITH **ARTIFICIAL SNOW** TO KEEP THEM FROM **SHRINKING.**

124

CITY BIRDS ARE BETTER AT SOLVING PROBLEMS THAN **COUNTRY BIRDS,** A STUDY FOUND.

THE WORLD'S **FASTEST FLYING** CREATURE IS A

BAT.

The **Sand Museum** in Tottori, Japan, featured a **model** of MOUNT RUSHMORE crafted from about

3,000 tons
(2,722 t) **OF SAND.**

Doctors once found **150 worms** living inside a woman's stomach.

NAKED MOLE RATS CAN SURVIVE WITHOUT OXYGEN FOR 18 MINUTES.

That's Weird!

POODLES ARE **BANNED** FROM COMPETING IN THE **IDITAROD.**

The world's heaviest **turnip** weighed as much as a four-year-old **kid.**

THE AVERAGE AMERICAN EATS ABOUT A TON OF FOOD EACH YEAR. (0.9 t)

SCIENTISTS MADE A BATTERY USING **MUSHROOMS.**

The largest **muscle** in your body is your **gluteus maximus**— in your rear end.

127

An Australian man once tried to auction off the country of New Zealand online.

Too much **oxygen** can make **you** **sick.**

GRAB A BITE IN ONE OF THESE U.S. TOWNS:

OATMEAL, TEXAS

SANDWICH, MASSACHUSETTS

PIE TOWN, NEW MEXICO

BURNT CORN, ALABAMA

CHICKEN, ALASKA

COOKIETOWN, OKLAHOMA

You become temporarily **paralyzed** while you dream.

275 PEOPLE FIT INSIDE THE WORLD'S LARGEST SOAP BUBBLE.

HORSES DON'T THROW UP.

THE **SNICKERS BAR** WAS NAMED AFTER A HORSE.

Starburst candies were invented in the **United Kingdom** and were originally called **Opal Fruits.**

spitters *sneesl* *snaw*

THERE ARE MORE THAN
400 WORDS FOR SNOW
IN SCOTLAND.

flindrikin *skelf* *unbrak* *feefle*

OCTOBER 9 IS NATIONAL MOLDY

★ ★ ★

CHEESE DAY IN THE U.S.

An ancient *Chinese warrior* is said to have **stunned enemy troops** *into retreat by* *juggling nine balls* at once.

MYANMAR, LIBERIA, AND THE UNITED STATES
ARE THE ONLY COUNTRIES IN THE WORLD THAT HAVEN'T ADOPTED THE METRIC SYSTEM.

U.S. PRESIDENT BARACK OBAMA'S
DOG BO IS FEATURED ON
A BASEBALL CARD.

Scientists found **sharks** living in an underwater **volcano.**

The entire land area of the **United States** could fit in the **Sahara desert.**

Some people
in Ontario, Canada,
ice-skate
to work.

44,000 CANS OF SPAM ARE MADE EVERY HOUR.

PILOTS AND COPILOTS EAT DIFFERENT FOOD OFF THE IN-FLIGHT MENU IN CASE ONE OF THE MEALS MAKES THEM SICK.

Americans renamed sauerkraut "Liberty Cabbage" during World War I.

A WOMAN IN CHINA GREW HER **HAIR** THREE TIMES **LONGER** THAN SHE WAS **TALL.**

AN ANCIENT **FLYING REPTILE** HAD A WINGSPAN ABOUT AS WIDE AS A **FIGHTER JET.**

Chocolate comes from a fruit tree.

Arica, Chile, once went **14 years** with no **rainfall.**

New England clam chowder is the official state dish of Massachusetts, U.S.A.

The **oldest** **pieces of** **paper** in the world are **4,600** years old.

If you ate **one variety** of **apple per day,** it would take you almost **20 years** to try all the **different kinds.**

AMERICANS WILL EAT MORE THAN **6,000 PIECES OF PIZZA** IN A LIFETIME.

The country of Tonga once had banana-shaped postage stamps.

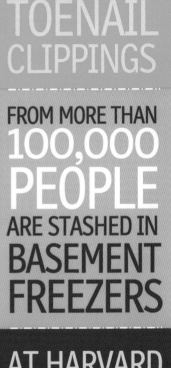

TOENAIL CLIPPINGS

FROM MORE THAN **100,000 PEOPLE** ARE STASHED IN **BASEMENT FREEZERS**

AT HARVARD UNIVERSITY.

AN ARTIST ONCE RE-CREATED THE "MONA LISA" USING ONLY PIECES OF TOAST.

"EMOTION RECOGNITION" SOFTWARE DETERMINED THAT THE "MONA LISA" IS 83 PERCENT HAPPY, 9 PERCENT DISGUSTED, 6 PERCENT FEARFUL, AND 2 PERCENT ANGRY.

The **50-star American flag** was designed by a high school student. His teacher gave him a **B minus.**

DISNEYLAND, IN CALIFORNIA, U.S.A., IS BIGGER THAN THE WORLD'S SMALLEST COUNTRY.

SOME OF THE BIGGEST PYRAMIDS

IN THE WORLD ARE IN MEXICO.

◀ A MAYA PYRAMID IN CHIAPAS, MEXICO

149

A STUDY FOUND THAT PEOPLE CAN'T ALWAYS TELL WHICH OF THEIR **TOES** IS BEING **TOUCHED.**

YOU FORGET MOST OF YOUR DREAMS.

A woman in England dug up a **potato** shaped like a duck.

quack

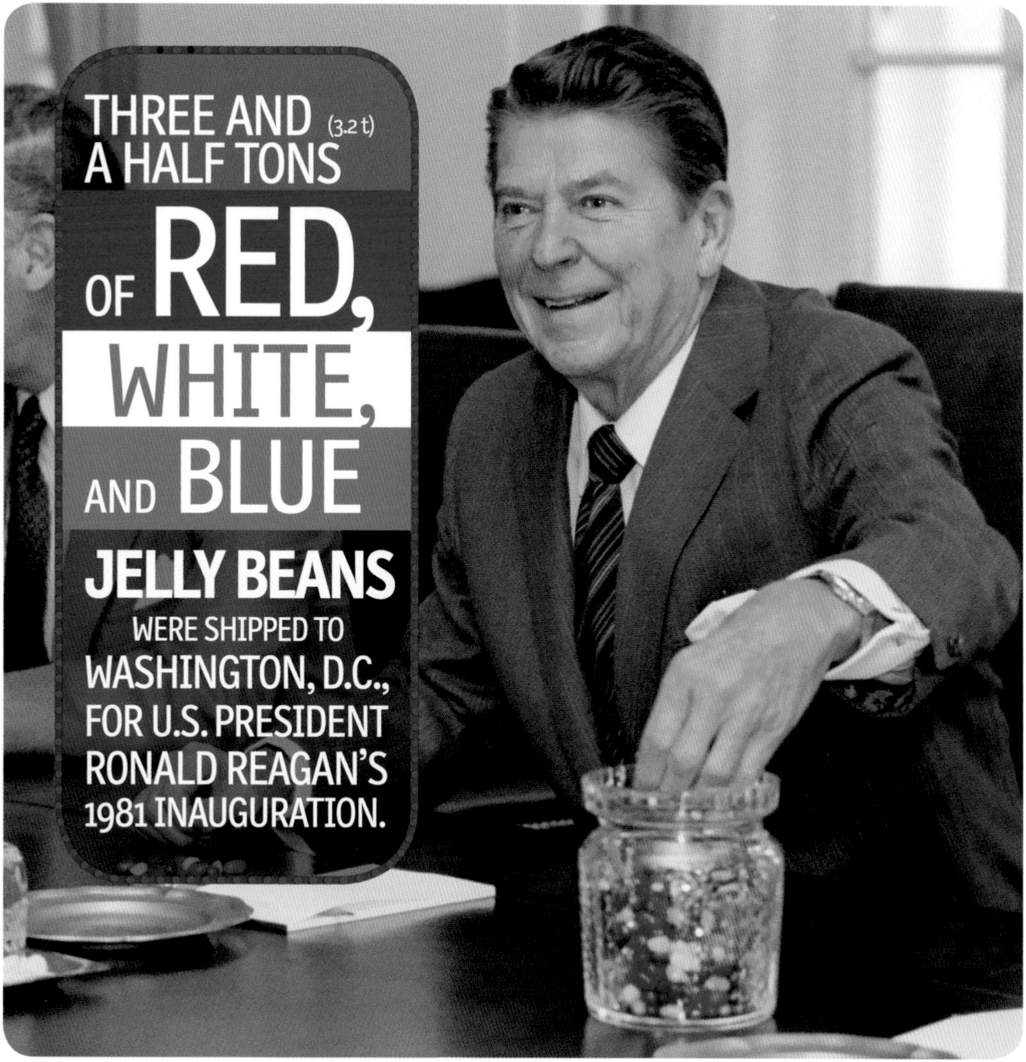

THREE AND A HALF TONS (3.2 t)

OF **RED, WHITE, AND BLUE**

JELLY BEANS WERE SHIPPED TO WASHINGTON, D.C., FOR U.S. PRESIDENT RONALD REAGAN'S 1981 INAUGURATION.

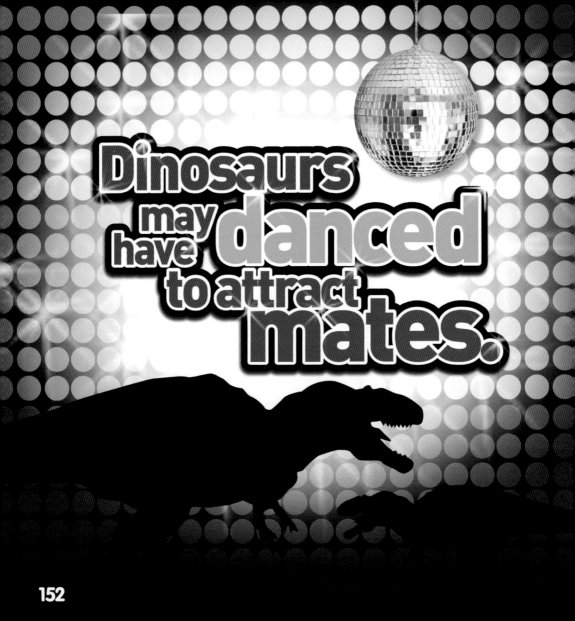

Dinosaurs may have **danced** to attract **mates.**

Some **turtles** **glow** in the dark.

PINK LEMONADE
WAS INVENTED BY ACCIDENT,
WHEN A LEMONADE SELLER DROPPED
RED CINNAMON CANDIES
INTO HIS LEMONADE,
TURNING IT **PINK.**

Octopuses have blue blood.

OCTOPUSES HAVE **NINE** BRAINS.

Giraffes hum at night.

Hershey's Kisses are said to be named after the sound they once made during manufacturing.

SCIENTISTS FOUND 2.5-MILLION-YEAR-OLD FOSSILIZED PEACH PITS IN CHINA.

THE **WALL** OF A MEDIEVAL CASTLE WAS FOUND UNDER **A PRISON** IN ENGLAND.

ONE AIRPLANE CAN CONTAIN 330 MILES OF WIRES. (531 km)

A fast-food chain once sold a **hamburger** that turned people's poop **green.**

More than 500 different types **of bugs** may be living in your house, a study found.

Microlattice— the world's **lightest metal—** is **99.99** percent **air.**

159

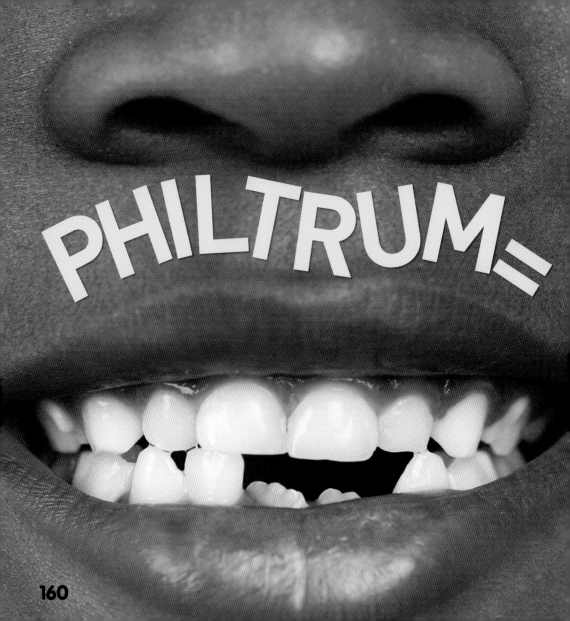

PHILTRUM

THE GROOVE BETWEEN THE TOP OF YOUR UPPER LIP AND THE BOTTOM OF YOUR NOSE

AUSTRALIAN SCIENTISTS MADE SWIMSUITS FOR SEA TURTLES.

A truck carrying onions once caught fire near Frying Pan Road in Texas, U.S.A. (The driver got away safely.)

A WHALE FOSSIL WAS FOUND ON TOP OF A MOUNTAIN.

Some people are paid to **sniff** out the source of disgusting **smells.**

SCIENTISTS HOPE TO **SEND AN ORBITER** TO **EXPLORE** THE SKIES OF **VENUS IN 2025.**

SCIENTISTS RECENTLY DISCOVERED AN EXTINCT DOGLIKE PREDATOR THAT LIVED AROUND

30 MILLION YEARS AGO.

"CORGI" IS WELSH FOR "DWARF DOG."

THERE ARE **12 SPECIES** OF **SPIDERS** THAT **EAT BIRDS.**

An **OCTOPUS** was washed into a parking garage **during a high tide** in Miami, Florida, U.S.A.

(It was rescued and returned to the ocean.)

Stethoscopes are also called " **guessing tubes**

MOST MAMMALS TAKE ONLY 12 SECONDS TO POOP.

SPACE HAMBURGER = THE DISK OF GAS AND DUST "FEEDING" A YOUNG STAR

People who regularly eat hot chili peppers **live longer** than people who don't, a study found.

The sentence "The five boxing wizards jump quickly" uses **every letter of the alphabet** at least once.

SCIENTISTS ARE **DEVELOPING** AN **ANTIBIOTIC** BASED ON **BLOOD** FROM A **KOMODO DRAGON.**

That's Weird!

CHIMPANZEES USE MAKESHIFT **FISHING RODS** TO **GATHER ALGAE** FROM RIVERS.

IT WOULD TAKE YOU ALMOST SIX MONTHS TO DRIVE A CAR FROM EARTH TO THE MOON AT 60 MILES AN HOUR. (97 km/h)

TURKEYS WERE CONSIDERED SACRED BY EARLY NATIVE AMERICANS.

THERE WAS A COCKROACH HALL OF FAME IN PLANO, TEXAS, U.S.A.

Blue is the most popular toothbrush color.

IT TOOK UP TO **SEVEN PEOPLE TO OPERATE THE GIANT JABBA THE HUTT PUPPET** FROM THE *STAR WARS* MOVIES.

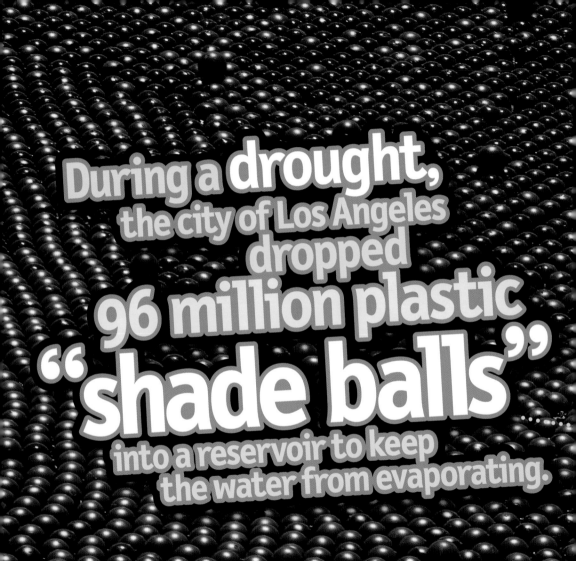

During a **drought,** the city of Los Angeles dropped **96 million plastic** **"shade balls"** into a reservoir to keep the water from evaporating.

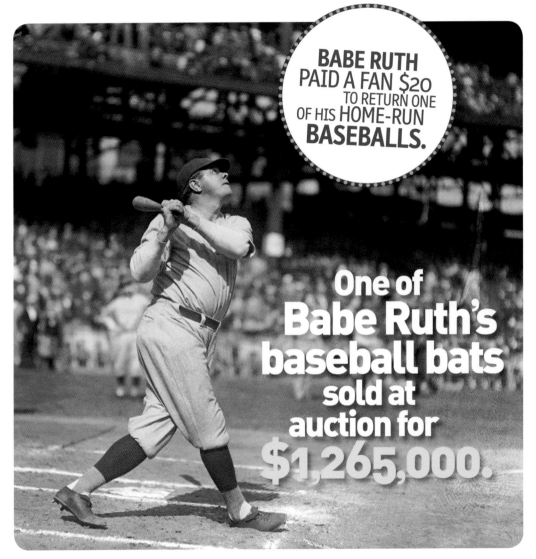

BABE RUTH PAID A FAN $20 TO RETURN ONE OF HIS HOME-RUN BASEBALLS.

One of **Babe Ruth's baseball bats** sold at auction for **$1,265,000.**

THE MOST HULA HOOPS SPUN AT ONE TIME: 200

A ROCK GROUP ONCE BANNED **BROWN M&M's** FROM BACKSTAGE AT THEIR CONCERTS.

SCIENTISTS HAVE TRAINED **PIGEONS** TO SPOT **CANCEROUS CELLS** ON MEDICAL IMAGES.

TAYLOR SWIFT TO BE DIFFERENT

DARE TO BE DIFFERENT

2015

A **FARM** IN MARYLAND, U.S.A., CREATED A **CORN MAZE** IN THE SHAPE OF SINGER TAYLOR SWIFT'S FACE.

SUMMERS FARM

AN ARTIST USED 17,625 GUMBALLS TO RE-CREATE TAYLOR SWIFT'S FACE.

Mantis shrimp send each other secret messages using light signals.

A lunch menu from the R.M.S. Titanic sold for $88,000 in an online auction.

In Massachusetts, U.S.A., it is illegal to dance to "The Star-Spangled Banner."

WORMS
THE SIZE OF
SNAKES
WERE FOUND ON A REMOTE
SCOTTISH ISLAND.

MOST OF EARTH'S SPECIES ARE STILL UNDISCOVERED.

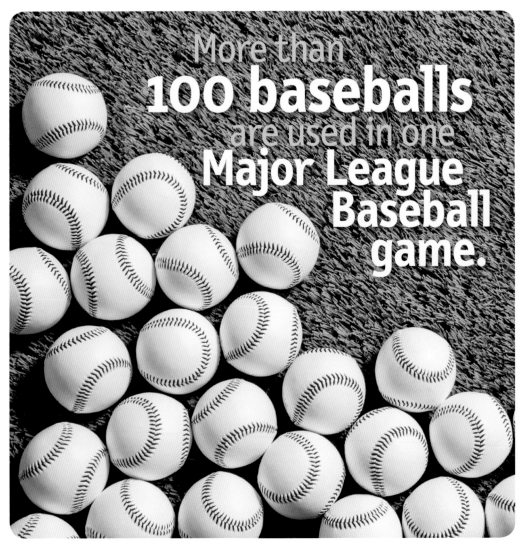

More than **100 baseballs** are used in one **Major League Baseball game.**

IT CAN TAKE UP TO **21 DAYS** TO MAKE A SINGLE **JELLY BEAN.**

YOU CAN BUY **EARMUFFS** MADE FROM **ROADKILL.**

Scientists found nearly **100 species** of **bacteria** **30,000 feet** (9,144 m) in the **air.**

A STUDY FOUND THAT CHILDREN WHO **GROW UP** AROUND **DOGS** HAVE A LOWER RISK OF **ASTHMA** THAN KIDS WHO AREN'T EXPOSED TO DOGS.

BY 2050 THE OCEAN WILL CONTAIN MORE PLASTIC THAN FISH, ACCORDING TO ONE REPORT.

MICROBES IN YOUR GUT TELL YOUR BRAIN WHEN YOU'RE FULL.

DURING THE **U.S. CIVIL WAR,** **LOLLIPOPS** WERE SOMETIMES MADE OF **HARD CANDY** STUCK TO THE END OF A **PENCIL.**

Scientists think that **Jupiter** bumped a **planet** out of our solar system four billion years ago.

A SCIENTIST USED MICROBES IN PETRI DISHES TO RE-CREATE A FAMOUS VINCENT VAN GOGH PAINTING.

The
South Pole
is the
sunniest
place on
Earth.

Scientists nicknamed a new species of peacock spider Sparklemuffin.

The Caspian Sea is actually a lake.

Spider-Man would need **sticky pads** covering **40 percent** of his body to be able to scale walls, **one study found.**

RESIDENTS OF BARNAUL, SIBERIA, CAMPAIGNED TO ELECT A CAT AS THEIR MAYOR.

The narrowest street in the world is only **one foot wide.** (0.3 m)

A KID HAD A LEGO PIECE STUCK UP HIS NOSE FOR THREE YEARS.

Cuttlefish hold their breath when **threatened** by **predators.**

AN ASTEROID NAMED SPOOKY FLEW PAST EARTH ON HALLOWEEN.

THE EARLIEST VERSION OF THE **PENNY** SAID **"MIND YOUR BUSINESS,"** NOT **"IN GOD WE TRUST."**

IT COSTS 1.5 CENTS TO MAKE A PENNY.

THE FIRST COMPUTER PROGRAM WAS WRITTEN IN 1842.

SCIENTISTS CAN USE AN ELECTRONIC TONGUE TO STUDY THE WAY FOOD TASTES.

JELLYFISH GOO CAN BE USED TO GENERATE ENERGY.

THE MOST SELFIES TAKEN IN THREE MINUTES = 134

SOME OF THE

first
vacuum
cleaners

WERE SO LARGE

THEY HAD TO BE DELIVERED BY A

horse-drawn •

carriage.

A dog drove his owner's truck into a lake in Maine, U.S.A. (No one was injured.)

Some scientists think the **moon** is a **broken-off piece of Earth.**

AN AVERAGE OF 12 MILLION **DUM DUMS LOLLIPOPS** ARE MADE EVERY DAY.

THE HAIRS ON RASPBERRIES

ARE CALLED STYLES.

The **land area** of the Riyadh, Saudi Arabia, **airport** is bigger than the city of Washington, D.C.

A commonly used **medicine** was developed from **mold** found in **sewer water.**

IT IS ILLEGAL IN SWITZERLAND TO OWN JUST ONE GUINEA PIG.

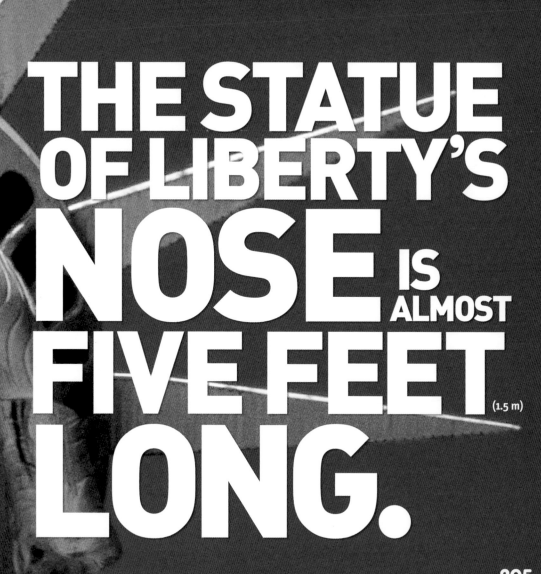

THE STATUE OF LIBERTY'S NOSE IS ALMOST FIVE FEET (1.5 m) LONG.

THE WORLD'S LARGEST COLLECTION OF FOSSILIZED POOP: 1,277 INDIVIDUAL PIECES.

THERE IS A GELATO MUSEUM IN ITALY.

IN CALIFORNIA, U.S.A., THERE IS A MUSEUM DEDICATED ENTIRELY TO **BANANAS.**

A MUSEUM IN OREGON, U.S.A., HAS A COLLECTION OF **300 VACUUMS.**

GUESS WHAT?

Sometimes even sticky syrup won't slow you down! **WHEN?**

Hanging around cows might keep you from itching! **HOW?**

WANNA FIND OUT?

If you want to cool down, yawn! **WHY?**

The FUN doesn't have to end here! Find these far-out facts and more in *Weird But True! 9.*

FACTFINDER

Boldface indicates illustrations.

FACTFINDER

FACTFINDER

FACTFINDER

214

All artwork by MODUZA DESIGN unless otherwise noted below:

Cover and spine, Eric Isselee/Shutterstock; 2, Eric Isselee/Shutterstock; 4-5, Pal Teravagimov/Shutterstock; 7, Marc Vasconcellos/The Enterprise; 8, yevgeniy11/Shutterstock; 10-11, EPA/DPA/Corbis; 12, Danita Delimont/Alamy; 13, All Canada Photos/Alamy; 16-17, Fairfax Media/Getty Images; 19 (background), Universal Images/Getty Images; 19 (UP), Ensuper/Shutterstock; 19 (LO LE), Christian Musat/Shutterstock; 19 (LO RT), Jnjhuz/Dreamstime; 19 (CTR), Aleksei Lazukov/Shutterstock; 21, djgis/Shutterstock; 22-23, Dave Watts/NPL/Minden Pictures; 24, Ethan Daniels/Shutterstock; 27, NASA; 28-29, FotograFFF/Shutterstock; 29, Isselee/Dreamstime.com; 30, Newcastle University, UK; 32, Jim Brandenburg/Minden Pictures; 34-35, irin-k/Shutterstock; 37, Yves Adams/Getty Images; 38, DM7/Shutterstock; 39 (UP), Sagamore Hill National Historic Site; 39 (LO), Sari ONeal/Shutterstock; 40-41, Toshi Sasaki/Getty Images; 42, iStockphoto/Getty Images; 44, Family Business/Shutterstock; 45 (UP), Adrien Nuñez/Shutterstock; 45 (LO), Eric Isselee/Shutterstock; 47, skydie/Shutterstock; 48-49, Donovan van Staden/Shutterstock; 48 (UP LE), Flickr RM/Getty Images; 48 (LO LE), r.nagy/Shutterstock; 52, NASA; 54, Sonsedska Yuliia/Shutterstock; 54-55 (background), iStockphoto/Getty Images; 56, Gorawut Thuanmuang/Shutterstock; 57, AlexussK/Shutterstock; 59, Michael Bahlo/Newscom; 60-61, Matej Divizna/Getty Images; 62 (LE), Zigzag Mountain Art/Shutterstock; 62 (RT), courtesy Todd Anderson/Autobahn Tuning; 64, Everett Collection/Shutterstock; 66-67, iStockphoto/Getty Images; 68, NASA; 70, Missouri History Museum, St. Louis; 70 (LO LE and LO RT), The Sun photo/Shutterstock; 72 (LO), David Lentz/Getty Images; 72-73, siambizkit/Shutterstock; 74, Friso Gentsch/Newscom; 75, Nathalie Speliers/Shutterstock; 76, National Geographic Creative/Getty Images; 77, courtesy Golf Cross France; 78-79, Retna/Photoshot/Newscom; 80, Djama86/Dreamstime; 81, Europics/Instagram/newspix.com; 82, MarcelClemens/Shutterstock; 84 (UP), Pavel1964/Shutterstock; 84 (LO LE), KYTan/Shutterstock; 85 (UP), Kodda/Shutterstock; 85 (LO), Odua Images/Shutterstock; 86-87, Cyril Ruoso/Minden Pictures; 89, iStockphoto/Getty Images; 90, iStockphoto/Getty Images; 92, iStockphoto/Getty Images; 95, Ron Gravelle; 96 (LO), iStockphoto/Getty Images; 96 (UP), PeskyMonkey/Getty Images; 97, courtesy of the Zoological Society of London; 98-98, Magda Sayeg; 100, Wendy White/Alamy; 102, SOMMAI/Shutterstock; 103, solarseven/Shutterstock; 104-105, Sarawut Kundej/Shutterstock; 106, Fiore/Shutterstock; 107,

NASA; 108, Volt Collection/Shutterstock; 110, Library of Congress Prints and Photographs Division; 111 (RT), photoDISC; 111 (LE), Dan Thornberg/Shutterstock; 113, SWNS Group/Newscom; 114, Bunpot/Shutterstock; 116-117, D. Trozzo/Alamy; 121 (LO), John Karmali/FLPA/Minden Pictures; 121 (UP), Dja65/Dreamstime.com; 122-123, Huguette Roe/Shutterstock; 124 (UP), DenisMArt/Shutterstock; 124 (LO), Genaker/Shutterstock; 125 (UP), SuperStock/Alamy Stock Photo; 125 (LO), National Geographic Creative/Alamy Stock Photo; 126, Kirkgeisler/Dreamstime.com; 131, courtesy Bubble Show by Mat j Kodes; 132, Rita Kochmarjova/Shutterstock; 133, ValentynVolkov/Getty Images; 134, Chuck Kennedy/The White House/Rapport Press/newspix.com; 135, Wrangel/Dreamstime; 136-137, Newscom; 139 (RT), Franco Tempesta; 140, iStockphoto/Getty Images; 141, courtesy Pierre Tallet, Sorbonne; 142-143, Food Centrale Hamburg GmbH/Alamy; 145, Maurice Bennett, Supplied by PacificCoastNews/Newscom; 148-149, Witold Skrypczak/Getty Images; 150, James Curley/REX/Newscom; 151, courtesy Ronald Reagan Library; 152, Olga Selyutina/Shutterstock; 153, courtesy Dr. David Gruber, National Geographic Emerging Explorer; 154-14, iStockphoto/Getty Images; 156, sergioboccardo/Shutterstock; 159, Photo by Dan Little, HRL Laboratories, LLC; 160-161, Blend Images/Shutterstock; 162, Courtesy Kathy Townsend, University of Queensland; 164 (UP LE), NASA; 164 (CTR RT), piotr_pabijan/Shutterstock; 164 (LO), Alexandr Mitiuc/Dreamstime; 165 (UP), Maks Narodenko/Shutterstock; 165 (LO), Eric Isselee/Shutterstock; 167, Everett Collection; 168-169 (background), AP Photo/Damian Dovargane; 169 (UP LE), AP Photo/Damian Dovarganes; 170, Bettmann/Corbis/Getty Images; 171, courtesy Edward A. Wasserman, University of Iowa; 172, courtesy J eff Greenwood, Summers Farm; 173, Rob Surette, Hero Art; 174-175, Whitcomberd/Dreamstime; 176, NHPA/Photoshot/Newscom; 178, Dan Thornborn/Shutterstock; 180-181, Marina Jay/Shutterstock; 183, BSIP/UIG/Getty Images; 184, David Aguilar; 185, courtesy Melanie Sullivan; 186-187 (background), Gen Productions/Shutterstock; 186-187 (CTR), visivastudio/Shutterstock; 187 (LE), Keith Homan/Shutterstock; 188, Jurgen Otto; 189, Anton Balazh/Shutterstock; 191 (LE), NRT/Shutterstock; 191 (RT), EPA/Newscom; 192-193, Melvinlee/Dreamstime.com; 195, welzevoul/Shutterstock; 198-199, Mary Evans Picture Library/Alamy; 202, Luke Sharrett/Bloomberg/Getty Images; 203 (UP), Nataliia K/Shutterstock; 203 (LO), Alptraum/Dreamstime; 204-205, 1999 EyeWire, Inc.

Since 1888, the National Geographic Society has funded more than 12,000 research, exploration, and preservation projects around the world. The Society receives funds from National Geographic Partners, LLC, funded in part by your purchase. A portion of the proceeds from this book supports this vital work. To learn more, visit natgeo.com/info.

NATIONAL GEOGRAPHIC and Yellow Border Design are trademarks of the National Geographic Society, used under license.

For more information, visit nationalgeographic.com, call 1-877-873-6846, or write to the following address:
National Geographic Partners
1145 17th Street N.W.
Washington, D.C. 20036-4688 U.S.A.

Visit us online at nationalgeographic.com/books

For librarians and teachers:
ngchildrensbooks.org

More for kids from National Geographic:
kids.nationalgeographic.com

For rights or permissions inquiries, please contact National Geographic Books Subsidiary Rights: bookrights@natgeo.com

Designed by Rachel Hamm Plett, Moduza Design

First edition published 2016
Reissued and updated 2018

Paperback ISBN: 978-1-4263-3118-3
Reinforced library binding ISBN: 978-1-4263-3119-0

Printed in China
22/PPS/3

The publisher would like to thank Jen Agresta, project manager; Avery Hurt, researcher; Jeanette Swain, researcher; Stephanie Drimmer, researcher; Kate Hale, project editor; Paige Towler, project manager; Julide Dengel, art director; Kathryn Robbins, art director; Ruthie Thompson; art designer; Lori Epstein, photo director; Hillary Leo, photo editor; Alix Inchausti, production editor; Anne LeongSon and Gus Tello, production assistants.